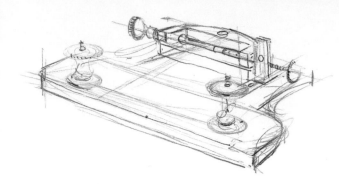

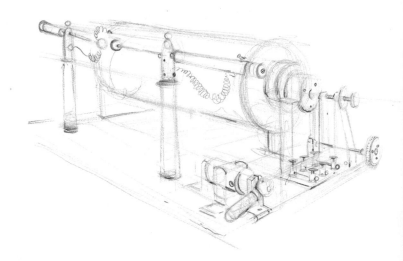

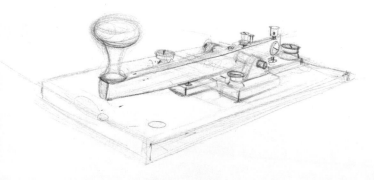

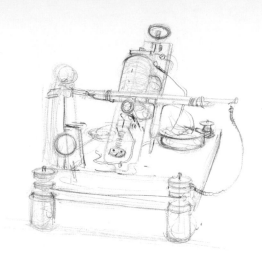

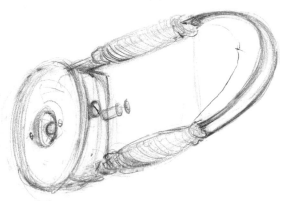

To Rachel, the budding radio engineer—BB
To the memory of George Kemp—RBC

First edition for the United States
published by Barron's Educational Series, Inc., 1996.

First published in Great Britain in 1995 by
Gollancz Children's Paperbacks;
A Division of the Cassell Group
Wellington House
125 Strand
London WC2R 0BB

Produced by Mathew Price Ltd.
The Old Glove Factory
Bristol Road
Sherborne
Dorset DT9 4HP

Text copyright © 1995 by Beverley Birch
Illustrations copyright © 1995 by Robin Bell Corfield

Designed by Herman Lelie

C·l 1999 14.95

All inquiries should be addressed to:
Barron's Educational Series, Inc.
250 Wireless Boulevard
Hauppauge, New York 11788

Library of Congress Catalog Card No. 96-83310

ISBN 0-8120-6620-0 (hardcover)
      0-8120-9792-0 (paperback)

Printed in Hong Kong
987654321

MARCONI'S
BATTLE FOR RADIO

Beverley Birch
Illustrated by Robin Bell Corfield

FOREST HOUSE ®
School & Library Edition

At the ship's rail the three men hunched down in their heavy winter coats. Icy winds blasted from the open sea, and they had to squint through sea spray as the ship nosed into the narrow neck of water toward the harbor.

At once they saw the great cliff. From its snowy rock, a tower gazed ahead to the harbor and back across the wilderness of the Atlantic Ocean where icebergs drifted like vast white mountains.

Was this the place where they could make their dream come true?

They did not ask the question aloud. Not a single person on that ship knew why they had sailed from England ten days ago, why they had crossed 2,000 miles of freezing winter seas to reach this distant corner of Newfoundland.

It was a secret, and they must keep it so.

The problem was that these three men were famous. People liked reading about them; at the slightest excuse reporters would take a ship or a train to track them down.

The three men weren't ready for that. Not yet.

And so they waited for the ship to dock, huddled in their overcoats, impatient to step ashore. First went Guglielmo Marconi, and then his two assistants, George Stevens Kemp and P. W. Paget, and behind them a strange assortment of luggage hauled from the ship's hold and piled on the dock.

Wooden crate after wooden crate, a huge
basket big enough to hold a large animal, but
light for its size, and long metal cylinders.

Across the ocean, on a faraway tip of
England, a group of specially chosen people
also waited, also impatient, to hear that
Marconi and his team had landed.

First, they must find the right place to work. Somewhere high. Somewhere with a view straight across the ocean toward England.

Somewhere like that hill at the harbor channel.

They all had a good look at it, particularly Kemp—for Kemp would have to launch the balloons and kites packed in that large basket. He trudged around, plodding through drifting snow. Was there room enough to anchor ropes for holding kites against this roaring wind?

Marconi and Paget hurried in and out of the old buildings. A splendid shelter for their equipment!

It was Friday, December 6, 1901 when they climbed that hill. It was bitterly cold and getting colder, and all the time they fought the fear that the vicious weather would never let them do what they had come to do.

We know their thoughts because they wrote about this day and the days that followed in their diaries. You can still read them today, more than 90 years later, and see how each of them felt.

Soon that hilltop echoed to the sound of pickaxes, as local men hacked at the frozen earth and heaved plates of metal around. Marconi, Kemp, and Paget raced to get their equipment safe and dry under shelter.

As they worked away on that icy hill, the twentieth century (the 1900s) was not yet two years old. There was no television or radio in 1901. Using electricity at all—for lights or machines—was still very new.

But people had learned to send a message
by electricity—as long as a wire carrying the
electricity joined the sender to the receiver.

No wire—no message.

That is, not until Marconi came along.

That was why Marconi was already famous. To the watching world he had conjured a kind of magic in the air above the earth. He had sent messages vibrating *through the air without wires*. No physical link joined sender to receiver, and Marconi's messages winged their way at the speed of light—186,286 miles each second!

Scientists had said it was not possible. They knew all about the mysterious, invisible electrical waves, and to think of sending them more than a few miles was just a dream!

It wasn't. Marconi had done it. He had sent the electrical vibrations into the air, as far as he wanted. He had caught them back from the air, just as he chose.

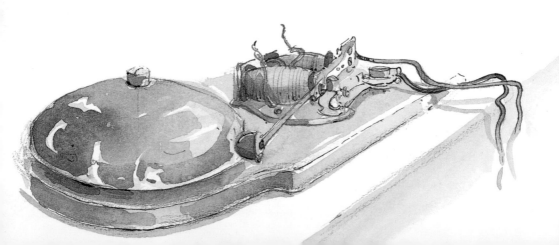

That was six years before, at home in Italy.
He'd only sent them from one end of an attic
room to the other, watched by his mother.

But months followed, while he fiddled with pieces of wire and metal. He struggled to make the vibrations jump longer distances between the equipment that sent them, the *transmitter*, and the equipment that caught them, the *receiver*.

His brother Alfonso became his constant helper, guarding the receiver, raising a shout of delight each time the surge of electricity sent by Marconi from the attic started the receiver's buzzer tingling.

First, Alfonso carried it down from floor to floor of the big house. Then out onto the sunny terrace. Finally, armed with a white flag to wave when the buzzer sounded, he marched away through fields and orchards.

One day Marconi had been trying out two metal plates wired to his transmitter. He arranged them first one way, then another, in the hope that he could make the signals jump farther. One metal plate lay on the ground.

By chance, he held the other in the air.

A sudden victorious shout! A frantic waving of Alfonso's flag! Far out of sight beyond a ridge, the buzzer   had buzzed.

The vibrations   had flown across hills!

A vast jump—just because of a metal plate held high in the air! Over the next six years Marconi worked and worked to get the arrangement right. He changed the air plate for a copper wire and called it an *aerial* (also called an antenna). The ground plate was the *earth*.

Week by week, month by month, he sent the electrical vibrations (now called *radio waves*) over longer stretches of land and water. By 1901 they could travel 224 miles.

Now Marconi faced the challenge of the Atlantic: 2,000 miles of unbroken water.

Again scientists said he could not succeed. They believed that radio waves moved in straight lines. The earth was curved, so (they said) radio waves traveling any distance would shoot out into space. The earth's curve between America and England made the bulge of the ocean like a water mountain 150 miles high!

But secretly Marconi prepared—first, a new radio station at Poldhu on the southwest coast of England, with a towering ring of poles to carry the aerials high into the air.

Next he explored a map of the world, tracing a line from the coast of England westward, across the Atlantic Ocean. He found the east coast of America, and searched for the best place to build a second radio station. There must be nothing but unbroken sea between the two.

Cape Cod. There, on the piece of land jutting out into the sea. Marconi and his team crossed the ocean and set to work. Slowly, the new radio station rose into the air—a ring of gigantic masts, just like Poldhu.

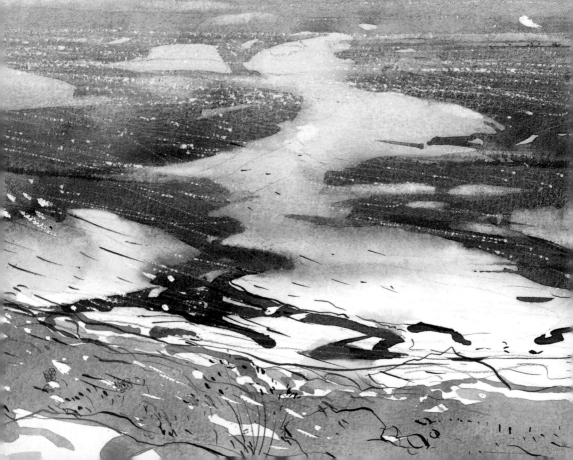

Then, disaster! Vicious winds tumbled the masts at Poldhu like matchsticks. The Poldhu men drew deep breaths, and began again.

But then gales roared through the aerials at Cape Cod and left a heap of broken wood and tangled wires.

So Marconi came to the snow-swept hill in Newfoundland named Signal Hill, bringing kites and balloons. His two grand Atlantic stations were in ruins, but it would not stop his dream.

Signal Hill also faced straight across the sea to England.

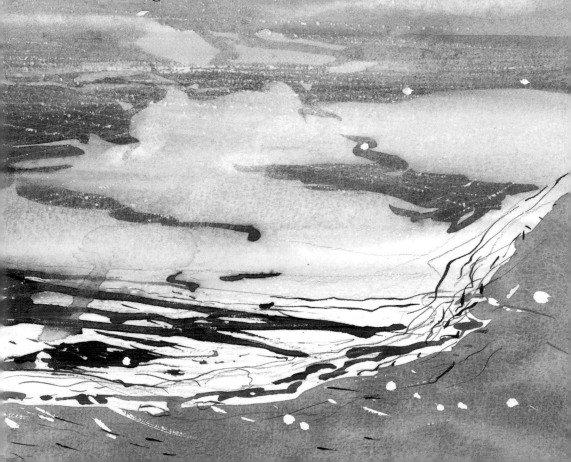

In England the team had rebuilt Poldhu, with lower masts to carry the aerials. These would send out the radio waves.

On Signal Hill, Marconi, Kemp, and Paget would try to catch them with aerials flown in the air on the balloon.

And now they were setting out the delicate equipment Marconi would use. The device to show whether radio waves had crossed the ocean was tiny—a narrow glass tube, no bigger than a thermometer. Inside were finely ground filings of different metals.

Usually the filings rested loosely in the tube. But if electricity reached them, they clung together or "cohered," giving the device its name—a *coherer*. There was also a little tapper attached—a tiny piece of metal to knock the tube and shake the metal filings loose again.

The coherer was linked to the aerial. When an electrical vibration touched the aerial, a burst of electricity ran down the wire to the filings in the tube. These would stick together and let the electricity pass across them—they formed a *switch*, switching electricity "on." At once the tapper would knock the filings loose and the electricity would switch "off" again.

But when no vibrations reached the aerial, the metal filings remained loose and the electricity stayed "off."

Usually Marconi connected the coherer to a Morse code machine. This tapped out short and long bursts of electricity as short and long sounds to show letters of the alphabet, or punched them as dots and dashes on paper. But at Signal Hill he worried that radio waves traveling all the way from Poldhu might arrive too weak to work the Morse machines.

Instead, he connected a telephone earpiece to the coherer; his ear might hear a click as each electrical pulse arrived and the metal filings clung together.

Trails of wire linked everything together, and led outside.

From there, Kemp would fasten one wire to a flying kite or balloon to form the aerial. Another wire linked the coherer to the metal plates that the local men had buried in the ground outside—these were the "earths." The process was called "grounding."

Through Sunday they worked on, testing, adjusting, testing again.

Monday came and went. The weather grew darker and fiercer.

Tuesday dawned. It was wet and foggy. But to their delight, the winds were milder—calm enough to risk launching a kite. It swooped and twisted, and Kemp ran to and fro—a guide rope loosened here, tightened there.

One whipped free and they rushed to trap and anchor it. A sudden slackening of the rope as the kite fell, then too sharp a wind tug, and a thick rope might snap like thin cotton thread!

The ropes held, and they had the kite safely in the air.

It was time to notify Poldhu.

They went down to the town and sent the message to England on the cable telegraph that lay along the bed of the Atlantic. Each day, for three continuous hours, over and over again, Poldhu must send out the same radio signal: the letter "S" in Morse code—three short dots. On Signal Hill they would try to catch it.

Wednesday roared in with storms, but they refused to let the weather stop them now.

They carried out the metal cylinders and released the hydrogen gas into one huge balloon. It began to inflate, swaying slowly off the ground.

Kemp wrestled with the guide ropes. The winds tugged at them, frantic, and the balloon tossed into the air, shuddering and vibrating.

Marconi lifted the earphone. Storm electricity crackled and hissed. The wind howled and the cliff thundered to the angry rhythm of the sea. How could he hear radio signals in all this?

Across the ocean in Poldhu the Morse code operator pressed a long lever—tap, tap, tap. At each tap, electricity jumped between two metal balls with a crash and a blinding blue spark. Out along the wires the vibrations traveled, away and over the wintery sea.

Could Marconi—2,000 miles away—possibly catch that signal a moment later?

On Signal Hill the balloon snapped at the ropes, watched anxiously by Kemp. Nothing in Marconi's ear but storm and wind.

Twelve o'clock came and went. One o'clock. Two o'clock.

Click click click!

Or was it?

Outside, Kemp used all his strength to tighten the ropes and hold the swaying monster balloon steady. If the aerials ripped off, they would have to start all over again.

Crack! The ropes snapped and the balloon shot into the air, lost among the clouds.

Now it was too dark and they were too exhausted to go on.

Thursday broke colder and grayer, with
lashing rain. They decided to try a kite this
time. They had six of them. If they lost these,
they would lose the battle.

The first kite wheeled and swooped like a
wild bird frantic to get free, and they fought
to stop it from plunging against the cliff.

Paget was outside now. Kemp and
Marconi took turns at the earphone.

Snap! The wind won. The kite whipped up
and vanished in the fog.

Out came the second kite, and up into the air, nearly taking Paget with it.

Marconi bent over the table, straining to hear. As the gale tossed the kite like a feather, the aerial kept changing height above the land and so changing its chance of catching any signals. It could never work in these miserable conditions!

Minutes ticked by. Not a single click in the earphone.

Was there something wrong with the instruments? Something wrong at Poldhu? How would they *know* if the problem was at Poldhu?

Paget hauled at the twisting kite, desperate to hold it steady at one height. The wind flung it away from him, higher.

A sudden click in Marconi's ear. He crouched over the earphone. The tapper striking the coherer! Electricity spurting down from the aerial!

Something was coming.

Three sharp clicks—close to each other. Unmistakable. The three dots of the Morse "S"! From Poldhu.

Silence.

He passed the earphone to Kemp. Kemp
listened. Nothing. Only the crackle of
the storm.

Click click click. Kemp *did* hear them!

They called Paget, but Paget was somewhat
deaf and heard nothing.

They listened again.

The kite soared upward and suddenly it was
the right height to catch the waves. Three
clicks in the earphone, then three more …
S-S-S-S … a whole series of them!

But still they kept the secret from the world. Just one more try. Just to be sure!

Hailstones and hurricane winds fought them the next day. Yet through it all came the dots—faint, fading as the kite circled, but always coming again, reaching them over and over.

Now they could let the secret out.

They told the newspapers on Saturday,
eight days after landing on Newfoundland.
In no more than the twinkling of an eye, radio
signals had traveled across the world!

And so those days of struggle against
Atlantic gales have gone down as one of the
great landmarks in our history.

There were many years of difficult work
ahead before they could give us the kind of
radio we have now—with voices or music from
anywhere in the world at the push of a button
or the turn of a knob.

But those were the beginnings—those icy
days on Signal Hill when Marconi, Kemp,
and Paget plucked the first "S" from the air—
and proved to the world that it could be done.

The rest is another story ...

Today, we can get information and entertainment by radio from anywhere in the world, straight into our homes. We can call for help across vast distances. Radio is a lifeline for anyone at sea, or in the air, or in any place where there are no wires to link them by electricity or telephone to the rest of us. Even the depths of the ocean and outer space can now be reached.

Before the beginning of the story in this book, there were many years of work on radio by many people in different places. And after Marconi's triumph, there were still years of work ahead, to give us the type of radio we now have.

It took Marconi and his team another year of work in Canada before they could successfully send signals back across the Atlantic Ocean, from Nova Scotia to England. They did not really know how radio waves traveled, and it was not for another twenty years, in the 1920s, that they found out enough to properly control the radio waves.

Then Marconi and other scientists had to learn
how to control the lengths of the radio waves
(called wavelengths). They had to develop
better equipment for sending
the radio waves (the
transmitters) and better
equipment for receiving the
waves (the detectors and
receivers).

A much better detector than Marconi's coherer
was invented, called a thermionic valve.
Eventually, this development meant that spoken
words and music could be transmitted, and not
just Morse code. Radio programs to entertain
people began to be broadcast in the 1920s.
And all the time, work continued on
sending radio signals over longer
distances. Short-wave radio was
developed, and in 1948 the
transistor radio was invented.
That was the beginning of
the kind of radio we enjoy
and use now.

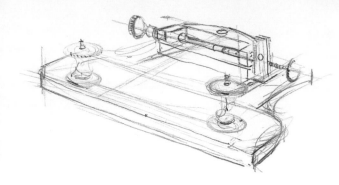

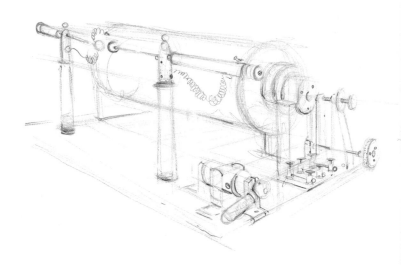

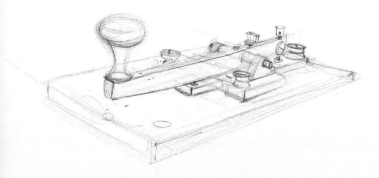

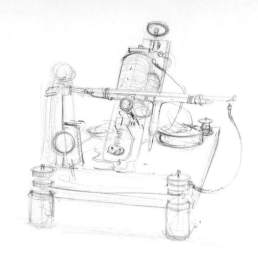

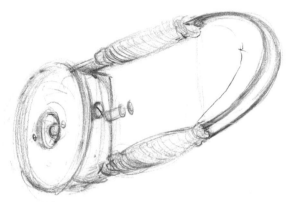

The Science Stories Books
by Beverley Birch

Benjamin Franklin's Adventures with Electricity
Illustrated by Robin Bell Corfield

Marconi's Battle for Radio
Illustrated by Robin Bell Corfield

Marie Curie's Search for Radium
Illustrated by Christian Birmingham

Pasteur's Fight against Microbes
Illustrated by Christian Birmingham

the two ruts which had more weeds than any well-used road would ever sport.

Thick trees lined the cart path.

Brambles pulled at her, tearing her clothes, slapping cold, wet splashes on to her skin.

Mud tried to suck her feet into the ground, but she kept running. But not fast enough. She couldn't keep up with Chalgrove's legs.

Breathing became harder, then almost impossible. She put a hand at her side and stopped, pulling herself free.

She let her breath catch up with her. 'I am not a race-horse. The briars catch on my dress.'

He pushed a limb aside and backtracked, stopping at her side. 'You're right to slow down. We'll have a break in the downpour eventually. But it's almost daylight. The ruts are hard to see in the dark and I don't want us to stray off the road.

'How will we…?' She tried to pull more air into her lungs and forced herself not to shiver. Water pelted down on her.

He held her, concerned as she struggled for air. 'I doubt she'll try to recapture us without her helpers. But we might stumble across her camp. We need to keep quiet, although they'll not be able to take us back. They can't have planned on us escaping and I can't imagine more than one guarding the place—or even one, in this rain.'

'I can't believe anyone's out in this. I know she isn't.' Miranda said the words without thinking and she didn't really know why she felt so certain except—except she knew that the old woman wouldn't be standing in a downpour.

She would be snug somewhere. In a cart with a stale oilcloth over her, or in another house nearby.

Miranda had lived in the house they'd just left. She

many imaginations.' He rocked back on his heels. 'They were not all imaginations. A few years ago, Wheaton told me he nearly broke his neck climbing that tree outside the window in the dark with a broom in his hand.'

'That was cruel of him to do to a child.'

'He really didn't like grass snakes. He'd told me they sent ghosts to people who caught them—after I'd put one on his shoes while he was wearing them. I forgot about the ghosts…when I found another snake. After two snakes, he took measures to make sure there wasn't a third.'

'I cannot imagine a servant acting so.'

'You have not met Hector Wheaton.'

He lay, listening to the scratches and scraping sounds she made. Every few minutes she would give a soft grumble, or groan or complain about the wood or the tool. Her squabbles with herself charmed him.

Night had fallen completely and he hadn't planned to sleep, but realised he had when her movements awoke him. The bed moved as she crawled between him and the wall. He'd never had a woman get into his bed so stealthily. For some reason, he found humour in her plan to enter the bed quietly. She might as well have jumped on it. Keeping the bed still was impossible. The light mattress moved like a dinghy in high winds.

He could tell she had positioned herself away from him and her body rested board straight.

If he tapped her side and shouted, she'd probably not stop jumping until she ricocheted off the ceiling.

He lay immobile, not wanting to let her know he'd awoken.

The governess soothed him more than any tavern songs, or boisterous friends or nights with his family.

She was delicate and yet not. A woman who'd walked

out of an uncomfortable life and made a new one that suited her better.

He didn't sleep, but lay there thinking about her as if she were a country away and a lifetime from him.

In the darkness, thunder cracked over the cottage and she jumped, wakening.

'Without thinking, he clasped her hand. 'It's just thunder.'

She stirred, but didn't speak.

The wind picked up again and the rain started softly, then increased, and drops pounded on the roof and into the room.

He rose, standing barefoot on a damp floor, and took a step where a puddle had formed. A puddle made from the leaks in the roof.

'Off the bed,' he said, jumping nearer her. He tugged her arms, lifting her to her feet and on to the floor.

With a heave, he pulled the bed, stationing it under the leak in the ceiling. He jumped on to the mattress again, gauged the strength by pushing with both palms, then with a fist, slammed the spot where the water ran in. The rotted wood gave way.

His hand could fit inside the hole he'd made and, in a matter of minutes, he'd rammed the remaining boards to and fro enough times to weaken them, showering himself in waterlogged splinters and the odour of rotting, wet wood.

Grabbing the largest piece he'd broken loose, he used it as a battering ram, increasing the opening. Pounding against the roof, cracking reverberated with the water rushing down. Water drenched his hair and rotted wood splintered as it landed on his cheeks.

He slammed the board upwards again, making a large

rupture. Water flooded over him as he opened the planks to the torrent above him.

He couldn't see the sky, but he could feel the freedom.

The opening had widened enough, but was slippery. He'd pounded away the damaged rot and found a strong section that he couldn't loosen.

Reaching up, he clutched the slippery boards, jumped and threw himself upwards. He climbed on to the top of the house.

'Toss up my boots,' he said, 'and put on your shoes.'

He grabbed the heels as she shoved them up and slid his feet into his boots.

'Let's go.' He crouched at the opening, lying on his stomach and reaching in to take her hands.

She lifted her arms and he raised her through the broken timbers with enough force that he had to roll and she sprawled over him.

'I could have planned that better.' He held her for a second, then released her. 'But I hope you don't mind that I didn't.'

He manoeuvred to give her a chance to right herself.

Standing, he tugged her hand, keeping her near. Water drenched them.

'Take care,' he said and steadied them, ignoring the pounding rain and concentrating completely on the task in front of him.

When they got to the edge, he didn't pause, but twisted and lowered himself, jumping to the ground.

'Now,' he called out, arms raised, and she tumbled into his arms.

He didn't give her a second to think, but gripped her hand and pulled her into the woods.

'Follow me.' He guided her among the trees, clos

should have kept in mind the direction to the nearest village, but she wasn't sure in the dark which way they should run.

He pulled her closer, under a large tree, shielding her from some of the rain.

'You're shivering,' he said. 'I didn't think it would be so cold for you.' Taking her hand, he sat and pulled her on to his lap. Wrapping his arms around her, he shielded her from the rain with his body.

'Your nose is cold.' But having his arms around her made her heart beat faster and filled her with warmth. She clasped his chest, snuggling tight, sharing his body heat.

The rain lessened, but neither of them moved, waiting until daybreak, sitting huddled against each other.

He dislodged her as the light began to shine around them. All the rain had stopped and the chaffinches began to call. Pulling her to her feet, he scouted the countryside and the fresh scent of the morning gave promise.

'I don't even know for sure which way to go, but we'll keep moving in the same direction.'

They arrived at a turn in the road, with a side path going away from it.

Chalgrove paused.

'It's that way,' she said, pointing.

Chalgrove stepped to Miranda's side. He put a hand at her shoulder, the smallest clasp, yet holding her motionless. 'When were you here last?'

'As a child.'

His eyes, intense, ignited her senses in the same way a spark flared gunpowder. She lowered her gaze, taking in the cheekbones, the column of his neck, finishing at the bristles of his beard. She could see the corded tension of his neck.

'I will find out.' His words left no room for doubt. She'd spoken to Willie in just the same tone when he had been caught outside with one of Polly's dolls ablaze and a lit candle at his side after he'd heard the story of Joan of Arc.

Chalgrove stood in front of her. 'You are better off explaining it from your point of view than letting me learn of it from a magistrate.'

'The fortune-teller spouts nonsense and curses and fables of unicorns. And when she talks in her sleep, I'd say she even lies then.'

'How do you know this?' He moved closer, so close she could scent the wet leather of his boots and the dry warmth of his face.

She couldn't meet his eyes.

'Don't expect me to be able to tell you her machinations. I can't.' She stepped away and her arm slid from his. She couldn't even fathom her own mind, much less anyone else's. 'How can I understand a daft old woman's intentions? I've not seen her from the time of my early childhood until she locked me in the room. She was old to me even then and she told my mother's fortune.'

His eyes narrowed. And she shivered inside.

Without speaking, he took off walking again.

She kept up until she got out of breath. Tugging on his arm, she caught his attention.

He stopped and, after observing her, took her to the wooded area beside the ruts and pulled her close, waiting. They were caked in mud and he embraced her, keeping her aloft, yet letting her rest.

'You know she will hang.' He dropped the words in the air and they formed images in Miranda's mind.

Miranda could feel her own feet dangling. Her father and stepmother had attended a hanging. Her stepmother had returned home with a whole basket of tales and had recalled the first vibration of the trapdoor, who stood where, what they were wearing and every utterance. The condemned man's last words had been repeated at least twice.

Soirées did not get as much attention.

'I know you want to have justice.' She closed her eyes, speaking softly. 'I am alive, though. I am unharmed and, should I be able to resume my duties, I want no more of this. I don't want to see the woman killed. She's addled. She must be. I have no coin to steal.' She pleaded, hoping to convince him. 'What good could come of her death?'

He reminded her of a stone wall, each rock chiselled into place so firmly it couldn't be moved.

'Satisfaction.' His brows creased. 'Others being safer.' A soft breeze blew through the leaves, chilling her, and he must have noticed because he pulled her even closer. Her palm flattened against his chest and he didn't feel like a stone wall any more, but more like a blanket.

She gazed up and found him watching her.

'If I were to leave this be, who's to say what she'll do next?' His voice was soft, gentling.

Miranda could hardly think to speak. 'I know she's addled,' she repeated. She clutched his arm, letting her hand rest on his sleeve, savouring the closeness between them. 'I know I should hate her. But I don't.'

'My freedom was taken. And nearly my teeth.'

She waited, trying to come to terms with the fate he intended for her grandmother, but she couldn't.

'Does it really matter to you?' Words spoken tenderly, but with something else beneath them.

Miranda didn't speak. He knew it did.

The knowledge caused her to waver and he held her. He rested his chin against her hair, embracing her.

'Let's move on.' Chalgrove spoke ever so softly against her hair. A pang of regret settled inside Miranda.

He released her, except that he clasped his fingers around hers.

His hair was finger-combed. The rain had caused his locks to curl around his ears. His shirt had lost all starch. His mud-caked boots were no more presentable than her shoes. He had passed needing a shave and sported enough hair on his face to begin a beard.

His eyes softened. In that moment, she knew he was going to kiss her. His mouth was nearer and her breasts warmed. She waited, lips parted, the moment bringing her body alive with yearning.

But he stopped and his mouth moved into a rueful smile instead of a kiss. He stepped back, his hand releasing hers. 'Forgive me, Governess. We'll have time to sort this out when we arrive in London.'

The sensations he caused didn't completely melt. But he'd called her Governess for a reason. He'd wanted to erase the attraction between them.

He looked into the distance. 'The magistrate will gather as many constables as it takes. I have the means to hire an army of men.'

It was as if he warned her.

All the warm sensations he'd given her evaporated.

Now, she just had to hope he never found her grandmother, or discovered their relationship. Not that her grandmother could keep anything quiet. A woman, who from the best of Miranda's recollection, never hid in the shadows and enjoyed calling attention her way.

Her grandmother had even complained when she'd had to stay inside the house, blaming the walls, the weather and, again, the stars…even in the bright of day—for bringing such a curse on her. The stars got credit and censure for everything that happened. But no magistrate would ever go after the stars.